In the Footsteps of Explorers

Hillary & Norgay

To the top of Mount Everest

x

Heather Whipple

Crabtree Publishing Company

www.crabtreebooks.com

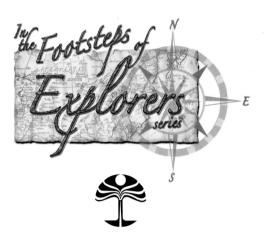

Crabtree Publishing Company

www.crabtreebooks.com

Coordinating editor: Ellen Rodger
Series editor: Carrie Gleason
Editors: Rachel Eagen, Adrianna Morganelli, L. Michelle Nielsen, Jennifer Lackey
Design and production coordinator: Rosie Gowsell
Cover design and production assistance: Samara Parent
Art direction: Rob MacGregor
Scanning technician: Arlene Arch-Wilson
Photo research: Allison Napier
Prepress technician: Nancy Johnson

Photo Credits: Peter Chigmaroff/Alamy: p. 28 (top); POPPERFOTO/Alamy p. 26 (top), p. 27 (bottom); John Price/Alamy: p. 29 (top); Royal Geographical Society/Alamy: p. 5 (bottom); Lee Karen Stow/Alamy: p. 24; James Sturcke/Alamy: p. 13; Andrew Woodley/Alamy: p. 25 (bottom); AP Photo/Binod Joshi: p. 30 (bottom); AP Photo/NZPA, Ross Setford: p. 18; AP Photo/Dave Watson: p. 20; Private Collection, The Stapleton Collection/The Bridgeman Art Library: p. 12; Royal Geographical Society, London, UK/The Bridgeman Art Library: p. 6, p. 23; Skekar Dzong, Tibet/The Bridgeman Art Library: pp. 12-13; The Worshipful Company of Clockmakers' Collection, UK/The Bridgeman Art Library: p. 11; Craig Lovell/Corbis: p. 14; Galen Rowell/Corbis: pp. 10-11; The Granger Collection, New York: cover, p. 8, p. 15 (top), p. 16, p. 19 (bottom right); Mary Evans Picture Library/The Image Works: p. 7, p. 21 (top); NMPFT/Hulton-Getty/SSPL/The Image Works: p. 26 (bottom); NMPFT/Kodak Collection/SSPL/The Image Works: p. 15 (bottom); Christine Pemberton/The Image Works: p. 22; SSPL/The Image Works: p. 19 (bottom left); Topham/The Image Works: p. 10; Paul Keel/Photo Researchers, Inc.: p. 17 (top left); Reuters/Gopal Chitrakar: p. 25 (top), p. 29 (bottom), p. 30 (top); REUTERS/Pawel Kopczynski: p. 28 (bottom); REUTERS/Stringer: p. 31 (bottom).

Illustrations: Colin Mayne: p. 4

Cover: Edmund Hillary (left) and Tenzing Norgay made the first successful ascent to the top of the world's highest mountain in 1953.

Title page: Ancient cartography, or mapmaking, was often not accurate.

Sidebar icon: Yaks are hairy cattle-like animals that are herded and kept for their milk, meat, and hair. Yaks also transport people in areas where there are no roads. Some yaks roam wild.

Library and Archives Canada Cataloguing in Publication

Whipple, Heather
    Hillary and Norgay : to the top of Mount Everest / Heather Whipple.

(In the footsteps of explorers)
Includes index.
ISBN 978-0-7787-2418-6 (bound)
ISBN 978-0-7787-2454-4 (pbk.)

    1. Hillary, Edmund, Sir--Juvenile literature. 2. Tenzing Norkey, 1914-1986--Juvenile literature. 3. Mountaineers--New Zealand--Biography--Juvenile literature. 4. Mountaineers--Nepal--Biography--Juvenile literature. 5. Mountaineering--Everest, Mount (China and Nepal)--Juvenile literature. 6. Everest, Mount (China and Nepal)--Juvenile literature. I. Title. II. Series.

GV199.44.E85W45 2007   j796.5220922   C2007-900665-5

Library of Congress Cataloging-in-Publication Data

Whipple, Heather.
    Hillary and Norgay : to the top of Mount Everest / written by Heather Whipple.
        p. cm. -- (In the footsteps of explorers)
    Includes index.
    ISBN-13: 978-0-7787-2418-6 (rlb)
    ISBN-10: 0-7787-2418-2 (rlb)
    ISBN-13: 978-0-7787-2454-4 (pb)
    ISBN-10: 0-7787-2454-9 (pb)
    1. Hillary, Edmund, Sir--Juvenile literature. 2. Tenzing Norkey, 1914-1986--Juvenile literature. 3. Mountaineers--New Zealand--Biography--Juvenile literature. I. Title. II. Series.

GV199.92.H54W45 2007
796.52'20922--dc22
[B]   2007003404

Crabtree Publishing Company

www.crabtreebooks.com   1-800-387-7650

Published in Canada
Crabtree Publishing
616 Welland Ave.
St. Catharines, ON
L2M 5V6

Published in the United States
Crabtree Publishing
PMB16A
350 Fifth Ave., Suite 3308
New York, NY 10118

Published in the United Kingdom
Crabtree Publishing
White Cross Mills
High Town, Lancaster
LA1 4XS

Published in Australia
Crabtree Publishing
386 Mt. Alexander Rd.
Ascot Vale (Melbourne)
VIC 3032

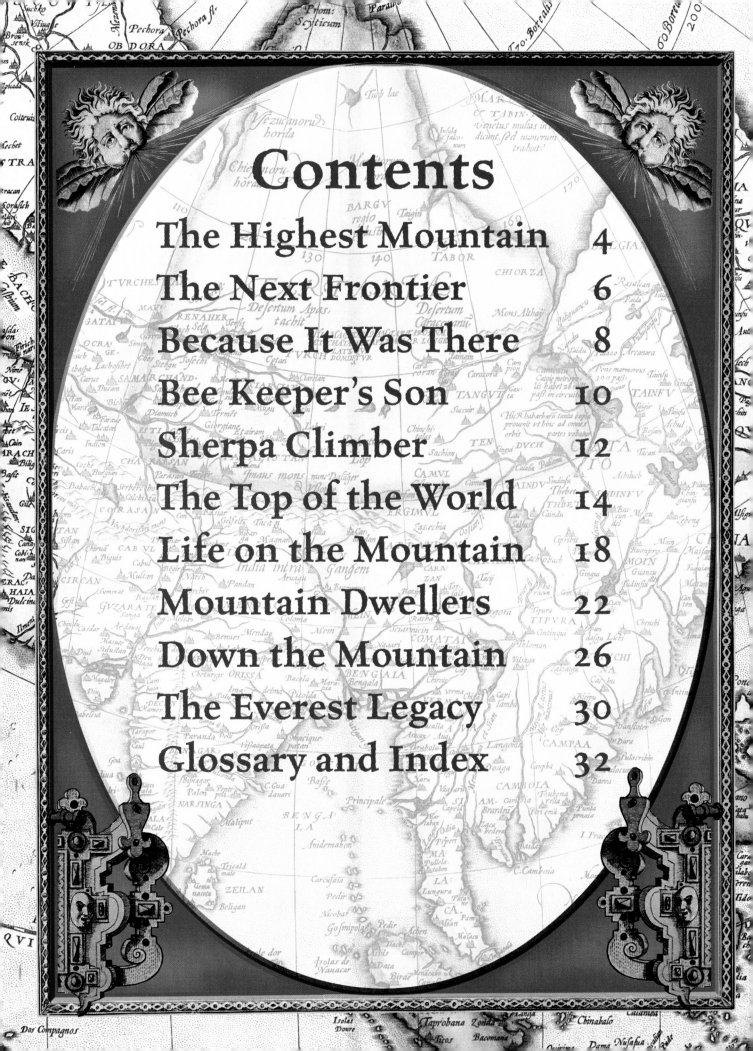

Contents

The Highest Mountain

Sir Edmund Hillary and Tenzing Norgay were the first mountain climbers to reach the top of Mount Everest, the highest mountain in the world, in 1953. Everest is one peak in the Himalayan mountain range that stretches across China, India, and Nepal. After their famous climb, both men worked to help make life better for the people of the Himalayas.

New Zealand Climber

Sir Edmund Hillary discovered his love of mountain climbing while growing up in New Zealand. After serving in the New Zealand Air Force during **World War II**, Hillary climbed mountains in New Zealand and Europe before his first trip to the Himalayas in 1951. After climbing the world's highest mountain, he worked with the Sherpa people of the Everest area to build schools and hospitals in Nepal. He also embarked on other explorations, including one to the South Pole.

Sherpa Climber

Tenzing Norgay lived in Tibet, Nepal, and India. He grew up near Chomolungma, which is what Everest is called in the Tibetan language. As a child, he dreamed of climbing it one day. His family was part of the Sherpa people, who live in the Himalayan mountains. He worked with many mountain climbing expeditions in the Himalayas. After climbing Everest, he taught mountain climbers from all over the world at the Himalayan Mountaineering Institute in India.

(above and right) Hillary and Norgay climbed as a team.

Higher Than Ever Before

Tenzing wrote about his life and climbing Mount Everest in his **autobiography**, *Tiger of the Snows*. In this section he described the experience of reaching the top of the mountain he had known his whole life.

> What we did first was what all climbers do when they reach the top of their mountain. We shook hands. But this was not enough for Everest. I waved my arms in the air and then threw them around Hillary, and we thumped each other on the back until, even with the oxygen, we were almost breathless. Then we looked around. It was eleven-thirty in the morning, the sun was shining, and the sky was the deepest blue I have ever seen.
>
> ~ Tenzing Norgay

(below) Tenzing and Hillary rest and have a warm drink at an Everest camp in 1953.

- 1856 -

Everest is first measured as the highest point on Earth.

-1914 -

Tenzing Norgay is born in Tsa-chu, Nepal.

- 1919 -

Edmund Hillary is born in Auckland, New Zealand.

- 1921-

The first group tries to climb Everest.

The Next Frontier

Everest and the Himalayan mountains have inspired people for many years. For the people who live in the region, the mountains are part of their history and religion. Outsiders have long been eager to discover how Everest compares to other mountains of the world.

Measuring a Mountain

The height of a mountain is defined by how high its **summit** is above sea level, the surface of the oceans around the world. Today we can use information collected by **satellites** to determine the exact height of a mountain. In the 1800s, scientists did not have such equipment. They calculated a mountain's height using careful observations and a lot of math. In 1856, the world learned that Everest was the highest mountain on earth at 29,035 feet (8,850 meters) tall. This means the top of Everest is more than 29,000 feet (8,839 meters) above the surface of the ocean.

Naming a Mountain

Everest is on the border between Tibet, now claimed by China, and Nepal, close to India on the continent of Asia. In Tibet, the mountain is called Chomolungma, which means "goddess mother of the world." In 1856, the British named the mountain Everest after Sir George Everest, the man who had begun the work to measure the heights of Himalayan mountains. More recently it has been called Sagarmatha in Nepal, which means "forehead of the sky."

The world's highest mountain was given the English name Mount Everest to honor mountain measurer Sir George Everest (above). Everest is called Chomolungma in Tibet and Sagarmatha in Nepal.

A Holy Place

The Sherpa people of the Himalayas and the Tibetans and Nepalese who lived near Everest, saw the mountain as a holy place and not something to climb. They believed that gods and demons lived in the higher elevations, and that people should leave them alone. It was important to protect the mountains and the animals there, to keep the gods happy. They also had legends of the yeti, a large, dangerous, human-like creature that roamed the snowy slopes.

The Next Frontier

People from other parts of the world, especially Britain, saw Everest as a new challenge. They wanted to explore all parts of the planet where humans had not yet been. At that time, exploration brought fame to explorers and honor to their home countries. The early 1900s saw successful expeditions reach the North and South Poles, two areas of the world that had never been reached before. Climbing the highest mountain was next.

radar

- J'AI VU LE YETI DE MES YEUX ! (Voir page 2)   N° 589 20 MAI 1960 60c
BELGIQUE 10 f. b. SUISSE 0,85 f. . MAROC 87 f.

An old European magazine cover plays up the Himalayan yeti myth by portraying a massive ape-like creature attacking a group of climbers on the slopes of a Himalayan mountain.

(background) Mount Everest is the world's highest mountain at 29,035 feet (8,850 meters).

Because It Was There

European mountain climbers in the early 1900s faced many challenges in the Himalayas. The countries in the region did not want outside visitors and the harsh climate was hard to get used to. Many climbers became ill from not having enough oxygen or from getting too cold. Still, they kept coming to Everest, dreaming of reaching the highest point on Earth.

A rock cairn was constructed in memory of climbers who died on earlier Everest expeditions.

Sightings of Land

At this time, the countries on either side of Everest, Nepal and Tibet, did not let visitors cross their borders without special permission. Great Britain ruled over India during this period, and Nepal did not want to fall under British control too. Access to Everest from the south through Nepal was closed until the 1950s. Getting to the mountain from the north, through Tibet, was also complicated. The Tibetan government granted permission for an expedition in 1920.

The First Steps

Before anyone could get to the top of Everest, they needed to explore the lower parts of the mountain. Climbers had to find good routes. In September 1921, members of the first expedition from Britain climbed 22,000 feet (6,700 meters), to the Rongbuk **Glacier**. In 1922, a British expedition climbed to 27,300 feet (8,320 meters). Before they could try for the summit, an **avalanche** killed seven expedition members.

Keep on Trying

Four more British expeditions went out in the 1930s. By that time, airplanes could fly to the Himalayas and aerial photographs provided information about new routes to the summit. Several British expeditions were stopped by bad weather. In 1938, the seventh British expedition reached 27,200 feet (8,290 meters) but could not get higher. By 1939, World War II had begun in Europe. For the next six years, the war put a temporary end to the British attempts to climb Everest.

Mallory and Irvine

One of the most famous British Himalayan expeditions was led by George Mallory in 1924. When a reporter asked Mallory why he wanted to climb Everest, he answered, "Because it's there." Mallory was a veteran climber who had taken part in the 1921 and 1922 British trips. He chose a less experienced mountaineer, Andrew Irvine, as his climbing partner. Mallory and Irvine never came back from their climb, and for years, people did not know what happened to them. In 1975, a Chinese climber spotted what was believed to be the body of Irvine on the mountain. An expedition in 1999 found Mallory's body. He is believed to have died from hitting his head in a fall. The expedition could not find a camera carried by the pair that would prove they reached the top in 1924. No one knows for certain if they reached the summit or not.

- 1924 -

George Mallory and Andrew Irvine die on Everest.

- 1934 -

Maurice Wilson attempts a solo climb of Everest and dies on the mountain.

- 1935 -

Tenzing makes his first expedition to Everest.

Bee Keeper's Son

Edmund Hillary loved being outdoors and began climbing mountains as a teenager. He climbed in his native New Zealand and the European Alps before getting to the Himalayas.

Adventure Stories

Edmund Percival Hillary was born on July 20, 1919, in Tuakua, New Zealand. His family kept bees to sell the honey, and his father also published newspapers and a magazine about beekeeping. As a child, Hillary loved adventure stories and movies, and he loved playing outside, having his own adventures. The first time he saw snow and mountains was on a school trip to Mount Ruapehu, in the center of New Zealand's north island. He was 16. By the time he was a student at the University of Auckland, Hillary knew his interest was not in his studies but in being active outdoors. Hillary joined a hiking group and spent many weekends climbing mountains around New Zealand.

Hillary developed a love for mountain climbing in his native New Zealand.

Climbing All the Time

When World War II started, Hillary volunteered with the Royal New Zealand Air Force and was sent to the south island of New Zealand for training as a **navigator**. He often had time to explore the mountains there. After the war, Hillary met Harry Ayres, a famous New Zealand mountaineer, who taught him the advanced climbing skills needed to reach the higher peaks. In 1947, the two climbed Mount Cook, New Zealand's tallest peak at 12,316 feet (3,754 meters).

Alps and Himalayas At Last

Hillary went to Europe in 1949 and climbed the famous **Alps** of Switzerland and Austria. When he returned to New Zealand, he was invited to join the first expedition from his own country to the Himalaya mountains of northwest India. Members of the group succeeded in reaching the top of Mukut Parbat at 23,760 feet (7,240 meters), but Hillary's feet got **frostbite** and he did not make it to the summit. That disappointment was followed by exciting news: a letter telling him he had a chance to join the 1951 British expedition to Everest. Hillary was already in the Himalayas and used to the thin air and cold. If he could bring his own supplies and meet the group in time, he could go.

A Path to Everest

The goal of the 1951 expedition was not to climb Everest but to look for possible routes from the south, through Nepal. Hillary and expedition leader Eric Shipton, climbed to about 20,000 feet (6,096 meters) where they saw a possible path to the top. They had no time to try it before winter snows set in, but the group hoped to come back in 1952. When they returned from the mountain, they learned they would have to wait. An expedition from Switzerland would get the next chance that year. The British team would not return to Everest until 1953.

(background) Everest's peak and Hillary's simple watch, used to keep accurate time on climbs.

Sherpa Climber

Tenzing Norgay had little formal schooling. He never learned to read or write, but he learned to speak many languages, which helped him in his later career as a guide for Europeans attempting to climb Everest.

Tenzing Sherpa

Tenzing was a Sherpa, a group of mountain people who farm and herd **yaks**, in the Himalayas. Sherpas follow the Tibetan Buddhist religion. Buddhists believe in reincarnation, or that when a person dies, the soul is reborn into a new life, over and over again, until the soul learns how to be perfect. Tenzing is believed to have been born in Tibet, where Buddhists also believe that gods and spirits live high up in the mountains. He had six brothers and six sisters, ten older than him and two younger.

Bound for Fame

Tenzing's parents named him Namgyal Wangdi, but a Tibetan lama, or Buddhist priest, told them he was the reincarnation of a wealthy man named Tenzing Norgay. The lama told his parents to change his name to help him have a good life. Tenzing later went to school to learn to be a lama but did not like it. If he had stayed in school, he would have learned to read the Tibetan language, but the Sherpa language was only spoken. It did not have an alphabet or writing.

A Tibetan lama holds prayer beads.
Lamas are important leaders.

Mountain Lover

When he was young, Tenzing was unusual among his people for his love of mountain climbing. Even though they lived in the shadow of the Himalayas, Sherpa people did not explore the mountains. Instead, they left them alone as places where the gods lived. His mother called Everest "The Mountain So High No Bird Can Fly Over It," and Tenzing dreamed of visiting it even as a child. He did not want to be a farmer, like his parents. Tenzing heard about the expeditions to Everest in the 1920s, he knew he wanted to go.

(above) Porters today haul heavy loads for trekking and mountain climbing expeditions.

Looking for Work

Sherpas who did not want to farm or herd yaks could find work in India on tea plantations or as **porters** and laborers. When European mountain climbing expeditions began, Sherpas were hired to carry equipment because they were used to the thin, dry air and cold weather of the Himalayas. There were few mountain roads and none large enough for cars or trucks. All supplies had to be carried on foot. Tenzing went to Darjeeling, India, at 18 to find an expedition job. He joined three expeditions to Everest before 1952. In 1952, he joined the first Swiss expedition to Everest, which reached 28,250 feet (8,611 meters) on Everest before bad weather forced them back.

The Top of the World

The 1953 Everest expedition was massive. Hundreds of porters and guides brought supplies to the Base Camp. From there, Sherpas inched up the mountain with the British climbers to set up the higher camps, sometimes making several trips in a day throughout April and May.

The British Expedition of 1953

Both Hillary and Tenzing were asked to participate in the 1953 British expedition. The two met for the first time in Kathmandu, Nepal, where the team gathered before hiking into the mountains. Almost 400 people left Kathmandu for the long hike to Everest on March 10. It took the group a month to reach Base Camp. On the way, they rested for several days at a Buddhist monastery high in the mountains called Tengboche Monastery. Tenzing requested a blessing for the expedition from the head lama at the monastery. This has now become a tradition for many climbers setting out to climb Everest.

Seasonal weather in the Himalayas leaves only two possible windows for climbing Everest: spring, before the monsoon storms, and fall, after the monsoons but before the winter storms. It is too dangerous to try to climb during the stormy seasons.

Setting Up Camps

Sherpas carried equipment up the mountain, a job requiring incredible **stamina** and skill. Most of the hundreds of non-climbing porters who reached Base Camp did not go any higher. For each of the eight camps higher up the mountain, Sherpas took many trips back and forth from the camp below to bring the required supplies up to each new level.

The 1953 Everest expedition members, including Sherpas and Tenzing, pose for a photograph. The mountain was climbed in May, when there was good weather.

Being a Porter

Mountain climbing expeditions use porters and guides to bring supplies and climbers up mountains. Some expeditions employ hundreds of porters. Each porter carries as much as 100 pounds (45 kilograms) of food, clothing, tents, and climbing equipment on his back. Portering is a form of cash income in the farming region of the Himalayas. Tenzing was the Sherpa *sirdhar* for the 1953 Everest expedition. This meant he was in charge of all the porters and guides.

Many early mountaineering expeditions set out from Darjeeling, India. Porters and expedition members walked 300 miles (483 kilometers) from Darjeeling to Everest Base Camp.

Working Together

On April 26, Hillary and Tenzing climbed together for the first time. That day they raced to break the record for returning from Camp II to Base Camp, and in the rush Hillary almost fell into a **crevasse**. If not for Tenzing's quick response to secure the line connecting them, Hillary would not have survived. They learned they were well-matched and shared a desire to be chosen for the climb to the summit.

Sherpas helped climbers dig steps into the ice and build rope ladders across cracks.

Who Will Go?

Expedition leader John Hunt chose which climbers would try for the summit. The plan was to have two attempts. Hunt chose climbers Charles Evans and Tom Bourdillon to go first, followed by Hillary and Tenzing. On May 26, Evans and Bourdillon climbed higher than anyone before, but they did not make the summit before returning exhausted. After a restless night at Camp IX, it was Hillary and Tenzing's turn. They awoke at 4 a.m. to check their equipment, eat breakfast, and climb to the top.

To the Top, at Last

Hillary's boots had frozen solid overnight, so he had to thaw them over the stove. He and Tenzing left the camp at 6:30 a.m., wearing all the clothing they had brought. They moved slowly and carefully up the steep slopes to a large stone "step" about 40 feet (12 meters) high. The step was later named the Hillary step. They climbed through a vertical crack in the rock and ice, their rope just long enough to reach the top of the step. They stepped up a few more feet and suddenly realized they were at the top. For 15 minutes the two climbers stood on top of Everest, the peaks of the Himalayas laid out all around them. The two shook hands and hugged. Hillary took photographs of Tenzing and of the mountains and sky all around the summit. Tenzing unfurled four flags tied to his ice ax, for Britain, India, Nepal, and the **United Nations**. He also said a prayer and left offerings of food in the snow for the gods. The climbers ate cake to celebrate before making the long climb back down to Camp VIII.

On May 30, Hillary and Tenzing returned to the rest of the expedition. A message was sent to Base Camp to let the world know what Hillary and Tenzing had done.

- March 10, 1953 -

The British expedition leaves Kathmandu (4,344 feet/ 1,324 meters).

- April 11, 1953 -

Base Camp is established at 17,900 feet (5,456 meters).

- May 29, 11:30 a.m. -

Hillary and Tenzing reach the summit at 29,035 feet (8,850 meters).

Life on the Mountain

Mountain climbing is difficult. When Hillary and Tenzing climbed Everest, mountaineering expeditions were not equipped with the high tech gear used today. If a climber fell or was injured, there was no rescue mission or search party with a helicopter. The injured person had to climb back down the mountain by themselves or face certain death from exposure to the cold.

Dry and Cold

High up in the Himalayas, the air is very dry. All the moisture is frozen into ice and snow. The bright sun reflecting off the white ice and snow can increase the risk of sunburn while also making it difficult to see because of the glare. The heart has to work harder to move blood through the body, and the very cold temperatures make frostbite a frequent problem. The **atmosphere** is thinner than at sea level, which means there is less oxygen in each breath of air a person takes. Headaches, confusion, loss of appetite, and difficulty sleeping are common at high **elevation**. Climbers need to drink a lot of warm liquids to help keep their body temperature up. They also wear sunglasses to protect their vision from the glare.

The extreme cold of the mountain can freeze skin and fingers in minutes. Frostbitten fingers turn black when the frostbite is severe and the blood supply has been cut off. Sometimes, frostbitten areas must be amputated, or cut off.

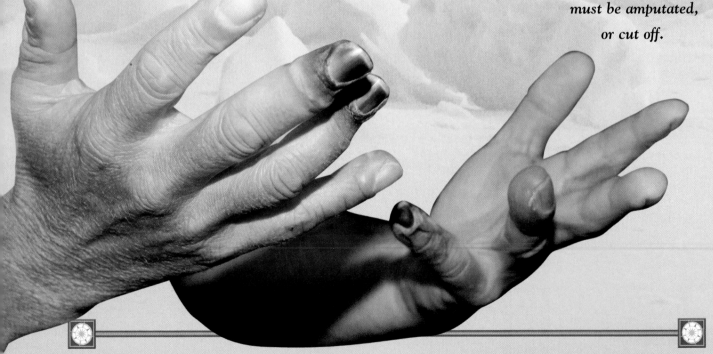

Don't Stay Long

Over time, most people can adjust to being at a higher elevation. Some people develop **altitude sickness**. The only cure is to move to a lower elevation. The expedition brought tanks of oxygen to help all the climbers sleep better. Hillary and Tenzing used oxygen on the way to the summit and back. It took weeks before Hillary fully recovered from the effort of getting to the summit.

Nothing Is Easy

Everything the team had to do was much harder than it was at sea level. Using oxygen from tanks helped them breathe, but the climbers also had to keep clearing ice that clogged the valves to the oxygen tank. They were less hungry and eating became a chore.

Climbers carried a lot of equipment, including ropes, axes, food, and oxygen tanks, which had masks that covered most of their faces.

The Ground Cannot Be Trusted

Every single step had to be checked for a secure placement before taking the next one. The icy ground was slippery, cracked and broken. Avalanches were a constant threat. For extra security, climbers were connected to each other with rope. If one slipped, the other could try to stop the slide. The changing conditions of rock, ice, and snow were also a constant danger. Every year, the landscape on Everest changes through **erosion** and from constantly moving glaciers. Air pockets, weak spots, and fractures posed problems even for the climbers who had been to the mountain before.

Altitude Sickness

High altitude environments, such as in the mountains, can make people used to low altitude sick. This sickness, called altitude or mountain sickness, happens because changes in air pressure and oxygen make it harder to breathe. Some people get sick only a few thousand feet above sea level. Others can tolerate much higher locations. Even Sherpas who were born and raised at high altitude may get sick if they spend too much time on the summit of Everest. Breathing less oxygen than the body is used to can cause many problems, including headache, loss of appetite, inability to sleep, exhaustion, and dizziness. People may also have trouble thinking clearly but not be aware of it. Altitude sickness can kill and climbers know that they must descend the mountain if they have symptoms. In 1953, doctors believed it would be almost impossible for someone to reach the top of Everest without using an oxygen tank. Not until 1978 did a climber reach the top "unassisted," or without using extra oxygen.

Mountain environments are so cold that dead bodies are preserved for years. This climber died in a rock alcove on Mount Everest in 1996. His body was discovered many years later by another climber who rested in the same alcove. People die almost every year trying to climb Mount Everest.

LA DOMENICA DEL CORRIERE

Supplemento settimanale illustrato del nuovo CORRIERE DELLA SERA - Abbonamenti: Italia, anno L. 1400, sem. L. 750 - Estero, anno L. 2000, sem. L. 1050.

Anno 55 — N. 24   14 Giugno 1953   L. 30.—

Conquistata la vetta del mondo. Una cordata della spedizione britannica, composta dal neozelandese Hillary e dalla guida nepalese Tensing, ha raggiunto, con l'aiuto di apparecchi respiratori ad ossigeno, la vetta dell'Everest (m. 8885) la massima elevazione della Terra, che aveva finora respinto dieci tentativi. Sulla cima sono state spiegate al vento tre piccole bandiere: della Gran Bretagna, delle Nazioni Unite e del Nepal. (Disegno di Walter Molino)

Hillary was drawn as a conquering hero in this Italian newspaper of the day. He never posed in such an outrageous manner on top of the world's highest mountain.

Life in Base Camp

Base Camp and Advance Base Camp were the largest of the temporary settlements on Everest. Everyone slept in tents, and they also used the tents as shelter during storms. The camp had a Sherpa cook, Dawa Thondup, who cooked both British and Sherpa foods. The expedition ate in a mess tent or dining tent. Drinking hot liquids is important for climbing under such dry, cold conditions. The expedition supplies included plenty of lemonade mix, cocoa, tea, and soup.

Rigi Koor (Sherpa potato pancakes)

Sherpas serve potato pancakes with yak butter and cheese. Yaks are a mountain animal similar to hairy cows. You can use regular cow butter and any cheese you like. Ask an adult to help you cook.

Makes 2 large pancakes
Ingredients:
4-5 medium potatoes
1/4 -1/2 cup (65-125 ml) wheat flour
2 eggs (optional)
chives, chili, salt for seasoning
butter to taste
Creamy, sharp cheese such as blue cheese

Directions:
Grate washed raw potatoes almost to a mash. Add enough flour to make a thick batter. The exact amount will depend on how wet the potato mash is. Add eggs for a richer batter if desired. Spread the mixture onto a hot, greased griddle or frying pan, spreading it out to the size of a plate. Cook over medium heat until each side is golden brown and crispy. Sprinkle with chili, chives, and salt to taste. Serve with butter and cheese.

Mountain Dwellers

The word Sherpa is from the Tibetan language and means "east people" because they came to the region where they now live from eastern Tibet about 500 years ago. Most Sherpas now live in Nepal and India, in the area south of Everest.

In the Shadow of the Mountains

Sherpas are **nomadic** herders and farmers. They tend herds of yaks in high pastures and grow crops of barley and potatoes in the short summers. Before Europeans first came to climb the Himalayas in the late 1800s, Sherpa people did not explore the higher regions of the mountains around them. For some, there were religious reasons to leave the peaks to the gods and spirits. For others, surviving day to day with few resources and difficult conditions was challenge enough.

Yaks are high altitude animals. They are kept for their milk, meat, and hair, which is used to make clothing and rugs. Yaks are also used to transport goods and climbing gear in the Himalayas.

Sherpa Language

The Sherpa language is a **dialect** of Tibetan, and their religion is a form of Tibetan Buddhism. Buddhist monasteries were centers of learning in remote Himalayan communities that had no other schools. Buddhists believe all life is sacred, and many do not kill animals for food. In the Himalayas, they use prayer wheels, metal cylinders that can spin, and prayer flags to send their prayers out into the world. Buddhists also believe that most people will be reincarnated, or reborn, after they die.

Tibetan Buddhists outside of a stupa, or dome shaped monument, at a monastery in Nepal.

Traditional Nepal

At the time of the 1953 Everest expedition, Nepal had few schools, hospitals, or roads. Most regions did not have electricity, radios, or telephones. Sherpas looked to the monks and lamas at Buddhist monasteries for leadership in daily life rather than to the government. In the Himalayan foothills, people lived in small villages with houses made from stone and wood. Their clothing was made of wool and leather from yaks, sometimes dyed bright colors and woven into striped cloth. Men and women wore long shirts over pants. Women also wore a striped apron. Today, western-style clothing is becoming more common.

Nepal

In 1953, the country of Nepal, where many Sherpas and other Himalayan peoples live, was a monarchy, or governed by members of a royal family. The capital and only city is Kathmandu. For the first half of the 1900s, the Nepalese government did not allow foreigners into the country. Expeditions to climb the Himalayas left from Darjeeling, the closest city in India, and crossed over to Tibet. By the 1920s and 1930s, some Sherpas and Nepalese people went to Darjeeling to look for work as porters for mountain climbing expeditions.

Sherpa Porters

Europeans first worked with Sherpa and Nepalese porters on expeditions in the Himalayas in the 1890s. Because the Sherpas lived most of their lives at higher elevations than most Europeans did, they were used to the high mountain conditions. Europeans had a lot of gear to carry, including supplies and scientific and technical equipment. Finding local help was almost always necessary. Some of the European climbers saw the Sherpas as servants, not partners on a team. Other Europeans developed close friendships and working relationships with Sherpas and valued their contributions.

(background) A Nepalese Sherpa stands before Mount Everest, in western Tibet

Their Reputation Precedes Them

Tenzing's accomplishment at Everest helped speed the change in how Europeans thought about Sherpas. Over time, Sherpas gained a reputation as strong, reliable climbers. This gave them higher **status** than other porters. Sherpas were hired as high elevation porters and guides, receiving more pay and better equipment for that work. Sherpas now hold many climbing records on Everest. The first person to climb Everest twice and the person with the most number of climbs (11) were Sherpas. The person with the fastest ascent from Base Camp to the summit (17 hours) was also a Sherpa. Sherpas continue to be important expedition members.

(top) Sixteen-year-old Temba Tsheri Sherpa, became the youngest person to climb Mount Everest in 2001.

(bottom) Buddhist prayer flags fly at Everest.

Down the Mountain

It did not take long for the news of Hillary and Tenzing's success to spread around the world. Both men's lives changed forever and the door was open for hundreds of other Everest expeditions in the years to come.

(above) The successful climb was front page news all over the world.

(right) At a cermony in 1953, Tenzing and Hillary were awarded medals for their climb from King Tribhuvana of Nepal.

Honors and Awards

Hillary and Tenzing were honored with many ceremonies and awards. Tenzing received the Nepal Tara medal from his own country, its highest honor. The climbers met the **prime minister** of India and the Queen of England. Hillary and expedition leader George Hunt were **knighted**. Tenzing was given the George medal for great bravery. Hillary wrote a book about the expedition called *High Adventure* that was published in 1955. The same year, Tenzing also published a book about his life called *Tiger of the Snows*.

Hillary After Everest

Hillary married Louise Rose in September 1953, and she accompanied him on some of his adventures. In 1954, Hillary was the leader for a New Zealand expedition to the Barun Valley, east of Everest. The next year, he was asked to lead the New Zealand members of a joint expedition to Antarctica and the South Pole. Hillary had been intrigued by Antarctica since reading about it while he was a soldier in World War II. Like climbing Everest, going to Antarctica required years of preparation. Hillary headed for the South Pole in October 1957. Five men drove three specially adapted tractors for 1243 miles (2000 kilometers) from a research base to the South Pole. It took over three months, but they arrived at the Pole on January 4, 1958.

Hillary's adventures continued after his Everest climb. He took part in other expeditions, including one to the South Pole, where his survival skills came in handy.

- 1963 -

Jim Whittaker is the first American to reach the summit of Mount Everest.

- 1975 -

Junko Tabei of Japan is the first woman to reach Everest's summit.

- 1978 -

Reinhold Messner of Italy and Peter Habeler of Austria complete the first ascent of Everest without oxygen tanks.

Tenzing After Everest

Tenzing traveled to Europe and throughout India after his successful Everest climb. He made Darjeeling, India, his family home and became field director of training at the new Himalayan Mountaineering Institute (HMI) in Darjeeling. The HMI teaches techniques of high altitude mountain climbing. Tenzing continued to go up into the Himalayas, but eventually his responsibilities in Darjeeling took too much time for him to join any major expeditions. After more than 20 years with HMI, Tenzing left to start his own tour company, called Tenzing Norgay Adventures, in 1978. The company organized tours, treks, and cruises around the world and is run by Tenzing's son today. Tenzing Norgay died in Darjeeling on May 9, 1986.

Schools and Vaccines

His trips to the Himalayas made Hillary want to give something back to the people of the area. He asked them what they needed and set about establishing schools for Sherpa children in the mountains. He also created the Himalayan Trust to help Sherpas get funding for projects they feel are needed. Hillary supported the building of small runways for Red Cross airplanes to land in the mountains and he also helped to set up a hospital and to bring vaccinations to the region.

The Himalayan Trust has built dozens of schools, medical clinics, and hospitals.

Tragedy and Recovery

Hillary, his wife Louise, and their three children visited Nepal and the Sherpa region many times. In 1975, Louise and daughter Belinda were killed in a plane crash near Kathmandu. After years of grief, Hillary finally found some comfort on a trip from the Indian Ocean up the sacred Ganges River in India to its source in the Himalayas. Hillary later remarried. He continues his work improving the social and environmental conditions in the Himalayas and lives with his wife, June, in New Zealand. In 2003, Hillary returned to Nepal to celebrate the 50th anniversary of his climb. He was greeted by cheering crowds during a parade in Kathmandu.

(below) Hillary's son, Peter, and Tenzing's son, Jamling Norgay Sherpa, made a successful climb of Everest together in 2003.

(above) A bronze sculpture of Hillary looking towards New Zealand's Mount Cook was placed in a valley below the mountain. Tenzing (opposite page) was depicted in a sculpture in Darjeeling, India.

The Everest Legacy

In the years following the first ascent of Everest, many more expeditions went up the mountain to try it again. Different routes, new equipment, and faster climbs were all tested. Today, Everest expeditions are no longer rare, and the mountain's popularity has changed the Himalayan environment.

Sherpa Income

The enormous increase in expeditions to Everest and other Himalayan mountains has made more Sherpas **dependent** upon portering and guiding for income. Sherpa ways of life have changed. Sherpas now have more money, better medical care and education, and more advanced technology. They also have more stress and more pollution in their homeland. Sadly, portering is dangerous and many porters still die in accidents on the mountain.

Trash on the Mountain

It will always be difficult to reach the summit of Everest, but it is now easier for more climbers to try. With increased climbing, comes increased pollution and more damage to the fragile mountain environment. Expeditions often left empty oxygen tanks and other trash on the mountain, not thinking about how it would accumulate over the years. Practices have now changed, but having so many people visit the mountain every year still has an effect on the landscape.

(above) A gold coin commemorates the 50th anniversary of the first Everest summit.

(right) Appa Sherpa, who has climbed Everest 11 times, inspects empty oxygen tanks brought from Everest Base Camp.

Deadly Preoccupation

In 1996, 15 people died on Everest, eight on the same day. Adventure trips had become so popular that 11 different groups were on the mountain that day. More than 20 people had reached the summit before a sudden storm hit the mountain, making it impossible to see where to go or how to help anyone down. Some people were trapped in snow or too weak to get down the mountain and no one could reach them to help. Others were blown down the mountain and killed. The tragedy raised questions about the skill of climbers and the quest to reach the top.

Adventure trips have made it possible for less experienced climbers to climb, which is not always good.

Each decade sees more people reach the summit of Everest.

1950s - 6

1960s - 18

1970s - 77

1980s - 183

1990s - 882

2000s - 1843 (est.)

Glossary

acclimatize The process of the body adjusting to conditions, such as weather and altitude

Alps A group of mountains in south-central Europe

altitude sickness A condition that affects mountain climbers when they cannot adjust to the amount of oxygen at altitude or high up a mountain.

atmosphere The gases that surround the Earth

autobiography A history of a person's life told or written by that person

avalanche A large mass of snow that suddenly slides down a mountain side. Avalanches can be deadly for people climbing and skiing on mountains

crevasse A deep crack in rock or ice

dependent Relying on someone or something

dialect A version of a language used in a specific region

elevation The height, or altitude, of something

erosion Wearing away of a surface, such as a mountain, through wind and water

frostbite An injury due to freezing

glacier An ancient compacted mass of ice that flows like a slow moving river over a land mass

knighted To be made a knight, a title of high rank in British society

monsoon A seasonal Indian Ocean wind that brings storms and snow to the mountains

navigator A person who directs a ship, plane, or other vessel to its destination

nomadic Traveling from place to place for food

porters People who carrry baggage and goods on their backs from place to place. Mountain porters carry goods up mountains

prime minister The head of government in a parliamentary government system

satellites Machines launched into space to do things such as observe weather patterns on Earth

stamina The ability to perform strenuous physical tasks for long periods of time

status A person's social position

summit The highest point

United Nations An international organization that promotes peace and cooperation between countries

vaccination An injection that prevents disease

World War II An international conflict fought mostly in Europe that lasted from 1939 to 1945

yaks Large hairy cow-like mountain animals that are herded and kept for their milk and meat

Index

Printed in the U.S.A.